Southern Messenger Poets
Dave Smith, Editor

CLAUDIA EMERSON

late wife

POEMS

LOUISIANA STATE UNIVERSITY PRESS

BATON ROUGE

Designer: Barbara Neely Bourgoyne
Typeface: Brioso Pro
Printer and binder: Thomson-Shore, Inc.

LIBRARY OF CONGRESS CATALOGING-IN-PUBLICATION DATA
Emerson, Claudia, 1957–
    Late wife : poems / Claudia Emerson.
        p. cm. — (Southern messenger poets)
    ISBN 0-8071-3083-4 (cloth : alk. paper) — ISBN 0-8071-3084-2 (pbk. : alk. paper)
    I. Title. II. Series.
PS3551.N4155L38 2005
811'.54—dc22

2005006033

I gratefully acknowledge the editors of the following periodicals, in which some of the poems in this book have appeared previously, some in slightly altered form: *Blackbird:* "Metaphor," "Pitching Horseshoes," "Possessions," "Surface Hunting"; *Five Points:* "Pond Turtle"; *Poetry:* "Artifact," "Daybook," "Frame"; *Shenandoah:* "Atlas," "Buying the Painted Turtle," "The Spanish Lover"; *Smartish Pace:* "A Bird in the House" (as "Something You Didn't Quite Want"), "The Last Christmas," "Leave No Trace," "Second Bearing, 1919," "Waxwing"; *Southern Review:* "Aftermath," "The Change," "Natural History Exhibits," "Rent"; *Tar River Poetry:* "Chimney Fire"; *Visions International:* "Migraine: Aura and Aftermath."

I also acknowledge with gratitude Poet Laureate Ted Kooser for awarding me a Witter Bynner Fellowship through the Library of Congress; the Virginia Commission for the Arts for an Individual Artist Fellowship; and friends and colleagues Marie McAllister, Ann Dickinson Beal, and R. T. Smith for reading many drafts of the manuscript. Once again, I am particularly indebted to my mentor Betty Adcock—who continues generously to challenge and inspire.

∞

 *for Kent*

All the forms are fugitive, but the substances survive.

—RALPH WALDO EMERSON

What else to say?
We end in joy.

—THEODORE ROETHKE

Contents

late wife

Natural History Exhibits

I.
Sometimes they used the hoe, or the dull blade
of a shovel, a stick of firewood, sometimes
the handle of the broom. I grew up around
women who would kill any snake, never
mind what the men said about moles and mice,
about markings or the shape of the head—
the good ones, harmless. Draping the body over
a low branch, my mother would claim, still breathless
from the killing, *rain, this will bring rain.*

II.
In this city's museum, beyond the rooms
of taxidermy, past the lit cases
of arrowheads and spearpoints, snakes are kept
in bright glass cells—a whole wall of them, a live
mural glistening, changing—the harmless
by the deadly. I recognize without
reading the sign the black rat snake; I know
already that it kills not by sudden
poison but wraps itself instead around
its prey, then tightens that embrace until it feels
the fear leave with the struggle, then the breath—
until the constricted heart grows still.

III.
It had to have come up from the cool underbelly
of the first old house we rented, climbing
pipes like branches to make a nest of the rusty
sink-cabinet drawer where I kept the silverware.
I opened it, and the snake lay coiled, brooding
on its bed of edges—blades and tines—
the hard bone handles, a wedding gift
from my mother's aunt. The snake never

raised its head. I hesitated, then
eased shut the drawer. Later, I would wash
every fork, spoon, and knife—and set the table.

IV.
I know now I should have killed the snake
and hung its long body as straight in death
as the glistening barrel of a gun. I was young,
new in my marriage-bed, but regret was already
sunk sharp in me. Like any blade, it would grow
dull slowly. The wound would heal around it
until its absence would cause the greater pain.
A good story, though, how I let the snake
escape, drain back into the house, and for years
I told at that same table what I had to tell,
how it disappeared the way it came.

I

divorce epistles

Aftermath

I think by now it is time for the second cutting.
    I imagine the field, the one above the last

house we rented, has lain in convalescence
    long enough. The hawk has taken back the air

above new grass, and the doe again can hide
    her young. I can tell you now I crossed

that field, weeks before the first pass of the blade,
    through grass and briars, fog—the night itself

to my thighs, my skirt pulled up that high.
    I came to what had been our house and stood outside.

I saw her in it. She reminded me of me—
    with her hair black and long as mine had been—

as she moved in and then away from the sharp
    frame the window made of the darkness.

I confess that last house was the coldest
    I kept. In it, I became formless as fog, crossing

the walls, formless as your breath as it rose
    from your mouth to disappear in the air above you.

You see, aftermath is easier, opening
    again the wound along its numb scar; it is the sentence

spoken the second time—truer, perhaps,
    with the blunt edge of a practiced tongue.

Photograph: Farm Auction

I have only one of the many
      images I watched you make
            out of your vigilant silence.

I am in it. You were documenting
      closure, you would tell me, one
            of many—the death of the small farm,

the small town, the way we had
      grown up there. In the hothouse
            of this frame, I have my back to you,

my arm around my mother's grief;
      the ribs of the umbrella are showing,
            sharp with rain. The auctioneer

points away from us, from you,
      as though sighting with relief the shore,
            his mouth paused beneath the loudspeaker—

a quenched, open morning glory,
      gunmetal hard. When you brought the image
            and this moment from their latency,

you called me into the darkroom
      to see what I had forgotten. You must
            remember how I admired the detail

of a hayfork lying flat in the foreground,
      angling toward the camera you had
            trained on it so that the many tines

are distorted, longer than they could
      have been—like a plate of baleen
            from the mouth of a whale, its rich body

harvested for something this small.

Rent

There were five houses over twenty years.
    We lived almost a decade in one,
        a mild, shallow winter in another.

We bartered work for rent in the last, the one
    that had already been let go. Privet crowded
        the porch, and a wall bowed into the parlor—abandoned

honey swollen inside it, the plaster crazed.
    We would share that house with swallows
        in the chimney, with the black rat snake

I'd find coiled in a basket of clothes,
    or stretched out on the bed. Bumblebees
        purred as though with contentment under us

and spiders—seasonless—survived the broom
    to live in every corner, their egg sacs hung
        like soft, spun pearls. Every spring, the bedroom

filled with termites flying, having come up
    from beneath the floor to mate and shed the brief
        wings I swept up like confetti; committed,

they returned to a narrowing crawlspace
    to feed their queen. I imagined her pale and thick
        as my thumb, invalid, being fed the house,

birthing more of what would keep her fed.
    When I worried the place would fall, you laughed
        not in our lifetime. That was true. It stood

those years where it yet stands, where you remained
    without me, living, you would claim,
        another, finer life, nothing the same.

But I imagine the walls still disappear inside
      themselves, vacant forms, and the house grows
           lighter, a deceitful ruin that lingers, rising

longer than it should above you and the fertile
      hunger that will, with enough time, consume it—
         before going on to another survival.

Surface Hunting

You always washed artifacts
    at the kitchen sink, your back
        to the room, to me, to the mud

you'd tracked in from whatever
    neighbor's field had just been plowed.
        Spearpoints, birdpoints, awls, and leaf-

shaped blades surfaced from the turned earth
    as though from beneath some thicker
        water you tried to see into.

You never tired, you told me, of the tangible
    past you could admire, turn over
        and over in your hand—the first

to touch it since the dead one that had
    worked the stone. You lined bookshelves
        and end tables with them; obsidian,

quartz, flint, they measured the hours
    you'd spent with your head down, searching
        for others, and also the hours

of my own solitude—collected,
    prized, saved alongside those
        artifacts for so long lost.

Waxwing

The cedar waxwing had to have
    fallen from some nest you couldn't
        see, so you brought it into the house

to save it. We fed it crickets
    sold boxed for bass bait, kept it in
        the cage we made of the kitchen—

where the bird sat on the sideboard
    for days—its mouth an insatiable,
        urgent flower—before finding flight,

the stalled blade of the ceiling fan,
    other rooms. For weeks we lived
        with the sound of wings. I grew

accustomed to the billing-purr,
    the feel of an electric, furious
        lightness clinging to my shoulder—

what it should have feared. The waxwing
    accepted us as given, and with us
        our seized, repressive sky, glassed light,

narrow stairway. So when we let it go,
    when it refused the atavistic
        sky, remained instead for one full

month in the hickory tree that loomed
    over the house, I asked you why
        we'd fed it. What had we saved

for a world so alien, the waxwing
    must have believed it had died in those rooms
        where for a while we went on living?

Chimney Fire

I learned to dread winter early,
        before fall showed any real sign
            of itself, the world still filled

with locusts, crickets, bees in the boneset,
        ashen moths quickening the dusk.
            Then around the time the hickory nuts

began to fall—the tree far larger
        than the house and fertile with sharp husks
            that struck, and struck again, startling

the tin roof and me beneath it—
        I began to dread as well
            the silence I knew would come yoked

to the cold. By then, you'd cut
        and stacked the wood, cleaned out the stove.
            In late afternoons, we scoured

the undergrowth for fatwood—skeletal sap
        for lighting the fire you rarely
            let go out. Every night you'd close

the stove down tight before we went
        upstairs, and the meager heat
            from that slow burn might keep the pipes

from freezing, but it wouldn't reach
        the bedroom where we slept beneath
            layers leaden as water that would not

float me, dense as mud beneath
        that water. In the morning, all
            our breathing had turned to ice,

blooming like white lichen on the insides
    of the windowpanes. One night, one winter,
        nearing spring, the fire would not

be kept; the chimney caught it, and we watched,
    heard it pour up into the tree
        the fire would have consumed

with the house, if it had burned much longer.
    But slowly the flames turned back, receded
        to the familiar—rise of smoke, banked coals,

my eyes, my mouth filled with ashes.

Eight Ball

It was fifty cents a game
　　beneath exhausted ceiling fans,

the smoke's old spiral. Hooded lights
　　burned distant, dull. I was tired, but you

insisted on one more, so I chalked
　　the cue—the bored blue—broke, scratched.

It was always possible
　　for you to run the table, leave me

nothing. But I recall the easy
　　shot you missed, and then the way

we both studied, circling—keeping
　　what you had left me between us.

Pitching Horseshoes

Some of your buddies might come around
        for a couple of beers and a game,
                but most evenings, you pitched horseshoes

alone. I washed up the dishes
        or watered the garden to the thudding
                sound of the horseshoe in the pit,

or the practiced ring of metal
        against metal, after the silent
                arc—end over end. That last

summer, you played a seamless, unscored
        game against yourself. Or night
                falling. Or coming in the house.

You were good at it. From the porch
        I watched you become shadowless,
                then featureless, until I knew

you couldn't see either, and still
        the dusk rang out, your aim that easy;
                between the iron stakes you had driven

into the hard earth yourself, you paced
        back and forth as if there were a decision
                to make, and you were the one to make it.

The Last Christmas

We were both sick. I had lost my voice;
    you were feverish, coughing. I had
        to split the kindling myself.

We'd been without power for two days—
    the spindling cedar darkening
        the room. The lines, still sleeved in ice,

sagged all afternoon above
    the arc of the axe, the lift and fall
        of the edge you made sure it kept.

It was late when I watched the blade
    graze wood and keep falling toward me.
        I felt it brush my pants leg close

as a cat, harmless. I quit then, certain
    I had let it fall where it wanted,
        not into seasoned wood but into me.

Surely, the ice would never melt,
    the pines would not straighten, I'd never
        speak. Later, when I carried up

your supper on a tray, you woke—
    pale, glazed from the fever breaking—
        and told me you'd worried when the sound

of splintering stopped. You were sure
    you had gotten up from your sickbed
        to look out that very window.

You said my mouth was open, but I was
    too far away and you could not hear me:
        I was small, mute beneath the window frame,

your breath forming, freezing on the panes
            until you could not see me,
                    and there was nothing you could do.

Metaphor

We didn't know what woke us—just
    cold moving, lighter than our breathing.

The world bound by an icy ligature,
    our house was to the bat a warmer

hollowness that now it could not
    leave. I screamed for you to do something.

So you killed it with the broom,
    cursing, sweeping the air. I wanted

you to do it—until you did.

Possessions

I sent you a list of what I wanted, and you boxed it up carelessly,
      as though for the backs of strangers, or for the fire, the way
      you might

have handled a dead woman's possessions—when you could no
      longer bear to touch them, the clothes still fragrant, worn,
      still that reminiscent

of the body. Or perhaps your lover packed the many boxes herself,
      released from secret into fury, that sick of the scent of me

in the bed, that wary of her face caught in my mirror—a thing I
      said then I didn't want, where I would not see myself again.

A Bird in the House

I thought that could be what it was
     to die, my body gone from you,

my voice, even my face, if alone
     in a quiet room you tried to recall it.

I was erased, but a stronger
     absence than death—even my name

disallowed, your new wife chasing
     it out, a bird in your house, something

you didn't quite want to kill—but would.

The Spanish Lover

There were warnings: he had, at forty, never
married; he was too close to his mother,
calling her by her given name, *Manuela,
ah, Manuela*—like a lover; even her face

had bled, even the walls, giving birth to him;
she still had saved all of his baby teeth
except the one he had yet to lose, a small
eyetooth embedded, stubborn in the gum.

I would eat an artichoke down to its heart,
then feed the heart to him. It was enough
that he was not you—and utterly foreign,
related to no one. So it was not love.

So it ended badly, but to some relief.
I was again alone in my bed, but not
invisible as I had been to you—
and I had learned that when I drank sherry

I was drinking a chalk-white landscape, a distant
poor soil; that such vines have to suffer; and that
champagne can be kept effervescent by putting
a knife in the open mouth of the bottle.

Frame

Most of the things you made for me—armless
rocker, blanket chest, lap desk—I gave away
to friends who could use them and not be reminded
of the hours lost there, the tedious finishes.

But I did keep the mirror, perhaps because
like all mirrors, most of these years it has been
invisible, part of the wall, or defined
by reflection—safe—because reflection,

after all, does change. I hung it here
in the front, dark hallway of this house you will
never see, so that it might magnify
the meager light, become a lesser, backward

window. No one pauses long before it.
This morning, though, as I put on my coat,
straightened my hair, I saw outside my face
its frame you made for me, admiring for the first

time the way the cherry you cut and planed
yourself had darkened, just as you said it would.

II

breaking up the house

My Grandmother's Plot in the Family Cemetery

She was my grandfather's second wife. Coming late
to him, she was the same age his first wife
had been when he married her. He made
my grandmother a young widow to no one's surprise,
and she buried him close beside the one whose sons
clung to her at the funeral tighter than her own
children. But little of that story is told
by this place. The two of them lie beneath one stone,

Mother and *Father* in cursive carved at the foot
of the grave. My grandmother, as though by her own design
removed, is buried in the corner, outermost plot,
with no one near, her married name the only sign
she belongs. And at that, she could be *Daughter* or pitied
Sister, one of those who never married.

The Change

My mother fought the house as if to rid
herself of it, spring cleaning without regard
for the season. She could drag the awkward bed
to the other side of the room and still have
strength enough to force the wardrobe out
so she could wash the wall behind it, its dark-

carved feet those of a raptor, its shelves layered
with linens embroidered in tight stitches,
her initials like scars risen pale in the healing.
And in the midst of all the scouring—beds stripped,
curtains down—she might at any moment
fling open the window as if to jump from it,

or fly. I understand now how she burned,
and some of why she rearranged those rooms,
so that she might wake and for once be surprised,
disoriented in that place as she was then
in her own body. In this way she fought the change,
her resolve as inextinguishable as the walls'.

Breaking Up the House

Every time I go back home, my mother
tells me I should begin to think now about
what I will and will not want—before
something happens and I have to. Each time

I refuse, as though somehow this is an argument
we're having. After all, she and my father are still
keeping the house they've kept for half a century.
But I do know why she insists. She has

already done a harder thing than I will
have to do. She was only eighteen—
her mother and father both dead—when it fell
to her to break up the house, reduce

familiar rooms to a last order, a world
boxed and sealed. And while I know she would,
she cannot keep me from the house emptied
but for the pale ovals and rectangles

still nailed fast—cleaved to the walls where mirrors,
portraits had hung—persistent, sourceless shadows.

House-Sitting

The first summer I was alone,
    I lived in a borrowed house
        in our hometown. I'd not yet broken

the habit of resorting to that
    place, though my belongings were
        already in another city

and I knew I'd be gone by fall.
    I had no phone. I would receive
        no letters—the temporality

that blunt. A house in transition,
    tall ceilings were made taller, grander
        by its emptiness. I slept

in a bed that, during the day,
    closed into the wall. The other
        rooms were bare, though the chandelier

still hung low over the place
    where a table would go, and the mirror
        behind it rose from floor to ceiling.

I was relieved there was nothing
    there to get used to. Evenings,
        I lit candles as though for guests

and danced with my own vanishing
    as the prisms moved in the draft
        my body made of the stillness.

Second Bearing, 1919

for my father

I have asked him to tell it—how
    he heard the curing barn took hours

to burn, the logs thick, accustomed
    to heat—how, even when it was clear all

was lost, the barn and the tobacco
    fields within it, they threw water

instead on the nearby peach tree,
    intent on saving something, sure,

though, the heat had killed it, the bark
    charred black. But in late fall, the tree

broke into bloom, perhaps having
    misunderstood the fire to be

some brief, backward winter. Blossoms
    whitened, opened. Peaches appeared

against the season—an answer,
    an argument. Word carried. People

claimed the fruit was sweeter for being
    out of time. They rode miles to see it.

He remembers my grandfather
    saying, his mouth full, *this is*

a sign, and the one my father
    was given to eat—the down the same,

soft as any other, inside
    the color of cream, juice clear

as water, but *wait, wait;* he holds
      his cupped hand up as though for me

to see again there is no seed,
      no pit to come to—that it is

infertile, and endless somehow.

Drought

I began to understand
      its severity when glassy

crows came shameless, panting at last
      to the birdbath, and when the locusts

fell to the ground, another failed
      crop. The street lay empty all day,

and the river grew thinner, its spine
      showing through. Only butterflies

thrived—the still air cleft by their
      repeating patterns, the feathering

wings of swallowtails, monarchs;
      I learned from their bright emersion

to rely, for a while, only
      on the eye, the dry horizon.

The Audubon Collection

The mockingbird, great white heron
    and screech owl hunt, mate, open

their mouths to scream; and the passenger
    pigeon is not extinct in this

framed, collective afterlife: Audubon
    was glass—invisible, exact

as God—into which they flew
    to be studied, perfected, to hang

on the walls of my house. He preferred
    to work from the dead; the certain

stillness afforded the intimacy necessary
    for this much detail, the captured-

alive too resigned or terrified,
    the preserved too perfect a lie.

(As a young man he'd been
    commissioned to make a portrait

of a child disinterred, and he had
    drawn a live likeness; even then

he could see beyond the mask.)
    He had to work quickly—often

drawing all night before the colors
    of the eyes and talons could fade, before

the advancing rigor. Dissecting some
    so that he might see what they'd eaten,

he sometimes cooked and ate one, declaring
    the herring gull "salty," the starling

"delicate." He killed countless
        for these portraits, his desire that precise,

that exhaustive. There will always be
        such things I regret knowing.

Still, in the margin before daybreak,
        when the darkness is unchanged,

but any chance of sleep lost,
        I can wake to their voices restored,

transfigured to one, distinctive, clear,
        but bodiless—in spite of everything,

rendered unrecognizable, beyond
        the walls—the window glass calling out

of something like despair, or hope,
        somewhere in the flightless trees.

The Practice Cage

I was taking my routine run, the same
      three miles just past daybreak on the jogging trail
           that encircled the playing fields—the home

of the Fighting Eagles. I'd run that course
      so many times I imagined myself
           a goat circling the invisible stake

of the baseball diamond's off-season
      desolation, scoreboard blank before
           the lightening sky. Behind the stands, I heard

first the dozen crows that crowded around
      a practice batting cage—a metal-framed,
           room-sized rectangle, its sides and ceiling

made of a thick, heavy net. Then I saw
      the cause of the complaint: a red-tailed hawk
           on the ground inside. I'd spent most of my life

in the country before moving to this city.
      I'd seen hundreds of hawks, but what I knew
           of them was distant patience, or an extreme,

diving speed, or death. I walked toward
      the cage, and the crows rose, scattered. The hawk
           flew up into the corner, struggled there,

twisting upside down as though tearing
      this other sky with his talons, before
           going limp, still turned, wings splayed outward.

Where I expected tension, fury, I saw
      instead the taming of despair—his eyes
           resigned to this, to me, softened somehow

as though with forgiveness. I could see where
        he'd flown in, one edge of the netting gapped,
                so I worked the knots to raise the hem

higher while the bird hung, indifferent
        to my effort, so motionless I was
                certain he was injured by the struggle.

But when I spoke, urged him, tugged at the net
        below, he seamlessly let go from that
                stillness, dropped down and righted himself into flight,

finding at once the wider gap—and was,
        with no wingbeat at all, gone, clearing the lip
                of the stadium to disappear into the turning

stand of poplars bordering the fields.
        I began my run again then, elated
                by the sound of my own breathing, by my feet

striking the ground beneath me, by knowing
        I would round that same turn, time after
                time, to see again in that familiar emptiness

something we had revised, an absence finished.

Atlas

In the museum gift shop at the foot
     of Marye's Heights, a lone, slim volume
          entitled *Orthopaedic Injuries*

of the Civil War lay remaindered
     at half price, a book many
          had handled without wanting to

own. I could not resist, either,
     looking inside, compelled by two
          photographs, portraits on the cover

of the same formal young man:
     in one image, both of his legs
          are missing; in the other, he wears

prosthetic limbs, bared for the camera.
     In image after image, the book
          catalogs particular survivals,

organized by the anatomic
     regions of loss: *extremities,*
          upper and lower, thigh, shoulder—;

some men are halved and in the next
     photograph risen from ether
          or chloroform, from opium

and whiskey, to wear inventions
     of wood, leather, metal. They had
          survived the bullet, the surgeon's knife,

and now this first, rough reconstruction
     of the body, to look past the aperture
          and into the photographer, wearing

the century's dark caul, then into me.
I bought the book, but not for their
unique disfigurements; it was

their shared expression I wanted—resolve
so sharply formed I cannot believe
they ever met another death.

Migraine: Aura and Aftermath

First, part of the world disappears. Something
is missing from everything: the cat's eye,
ear, the left side of its face; two fingers
from my right hand; the words from the end
of a sentence. The absence is at first
more absolute than whatever darkness
I imagine the blind perceive. Perfect,
without color or motion, nothing replaces

what is gone. The senses do not contradict. My arm
goes numb, my leg. Though I have felt the cold air
of this disappearance before, each time the aura
deceives me to believe reality itself
has failed. I fear this more than what it warns
because I cannot remember I will survive it.

The other half of me will shine all night,
defined by the eclipse.
                    Then, in the relieved
wake of the day that follows it, I will
find my hand, count my fingers, and beginning
to see again, will recognize myself
restored to the evening of a righted room.

III

late wife

LETTERS TO KENT

Artifact

For three years you lived in your house
just as it was before she died: your wedding
portrait on the mantel, her clothes hanging
in the closet, her hair still in the brush.
You have told me you gave it all away
then, sold the house, keeping only the confirmation
cross she wore, her name in cursive chased
on the gold underside, your ring in the same

box, those photographs you still avoid,
and the quilt you spread on your borrowed bed—
small things. Months after we met, you told me she had
made it, after we had slept already beneath its loft
and thinning, raveled pattern, as though beneath
her shadow, moving with us, that dark, that soft.

The Hospital

The hospital rises, a mute castle; walls
of impenetrable glass mirror the pall
of cloud and sky, give up nothing of disease
or the narratives of disease. We can see
it high above us, from the canal path, these wetlands
where we come to feed the turtles, where
the red-winged blackbirds purr and call, swelling
their coverts. You were with your wife up there

that last fall; you have told me how you looked
down on the narrow pier I thought we had
discovered, how even in her terror
she could still see to notice with pleasure
the bronze of the water, and these alders
before they lost to it the fat of their leaves.

Pond Turtle

You want to feed it; we both do. We have
come to know it well by its trailing veil
of air purling the water. This doesn't school,
and fish scatter before it. The massive
body just beneath the surface, it moves
the way your eye moves beneath a translucent
lid of dream. All is defense: the mud-
covered shell, the ragged blade of the mouth,

the head thicker than your clenched fist. Breaking
through my reflection, it displaces me as it feeds
on what we have cast here. It takes no pleasure
I can see; that is for us. Instead, it suffers our care
for it—and is perhaps relieved when the bread
is gone and when we can no longer see the breathing.

Daybook

This is the season of her dying, and you
have kept it, I find, underneath the stairs
in a box filled with photographs—her daybook
of that last year, the calendar a narrative
she did not intend to write. In the grid
of days, I see her habit had been to record
in pencil what might be erased, moved, saving
the indelible black for what could not change:

your birthday, hers, your anniversary. And in
that same decisive hand, the disease began
to eclipse this order, but she erased nothing.
Now from beneath the days the hospital claimed,
her first, latent words emerge, faint but certain
as images of ribs cradling milky lungs, the flesh forgotten
as water you can see through to the bottom.

The Cough

You can't recall when it first appeared in her,
but it must have been in late summer,
around the time the locusts came and muted
crickets, birdsong, the wind. And in the same way you
would not have perceived a tightening in the trees
before the onslaught of that sound, you noticed nothing
before it—fatigue perhaps, intolerance for the heat.
She kept saying then that it would pass with the season,

insisted, even as it consumed her, grew
bolder, not sleeping even when she slept.
It would outlive the locusts, but by days few
enough to count—the translucent forms still left
clinging to the world they had overset,
each one a perfect mold of the body that refused it.

The X-Rays

By the time they saw what they were looking at
it was already risen into the bones
of her chest. They could show you then the lungs
were white with it; they said it was like salt
in water—that hard to see as separate—
and would be that hard to remove. Like moonlight
dissolved in fog, in the dense web
of vessels. You say now you kept them longer

than you should have, those shadow-photographs
of the closed room of her body—while you
wandered around inside yourself as though
inside another room she had abandoned
to her absence, to barren light and air,
the one indistinguishable from the other.

Corrective

For a long time there would be the small
resurfacings of things you had forgotten
to throw away, or ceased to see at all.
These returned her, not to you, but to me
the way I had seen a spider unknot itself
on a warm late afternoon to move
again in slow relief—however brief
the hour, embolic, corrective—before fall resumed.

Homecoming

The camera is trained on the door, no one
in the frame, only the dog sleeping. And then
finally, I see this was to surprise you,
filming your arrival, the dog's delight. Only now,
six years distant, can this seem scripted, meant:
the long, blank minutes she waited, absent
but there—behind the lens—as though she directs
me to notice the motion of her chest
in the rise and fall of the frame, and hear

to understand the one cough, nothing, the clearing
of her throat. Then, at last, you come home
to look into the camera she holds,
and past her into me—invisible, unimagined
other who joins her in seeing through our
transience the lasting of desire.

Driving Glove

I was unloading groceries from the trunk
of what had been her car, when the glove floated
up from underneath the shifting junk—
a crippled umbrella, the jack, ragged
maps. I knew it was not one of yours,
this more delicate, soft, made from the hide
of a kid or lamb. It still remembered
her hand, the creases where her fingers

had bent to hold the wheel, the turn
of her palm, smaller than mine. There was
nothing else to do but return it—
let it drift, sink, slow as a leaf through water
to rest on the bottom where I have not
forgotten it remains—persistent in its loss.

Furnace

Just moved, we were still living out of boxes
when the old furnace refused another winter,
filling the house with oily smoke that woke us,
breathless. It would take them an entire
day to dismember and carry it up—
while the radiators' cold ribs rang, shuddered
with the sawing. All afternoon the deep
laughter of those rough surgeons rose up

from beneath the floor, the house grown rigid
with cold, while the blackened parts—dust flue and ashpit—
were piled on the street to be hauled off. The rooms
again would swell with heat, the house given
back to itself, ignorant of this warmth's new origin,
immune again, as we would never be, to the season.

Stringed Instrument Collection

You began it the third fall you were alone,
and soon they surrounded you: mandolins,
mandolas, guitars—cutaways, dreadnoughts—
the upright bass. You spent most of those nights
with the jazz guitar, learning Birdland and Twilight Time.
The others hung from inlaid necks, scrolled heads,
patient, mute, the way they hang now from
these walls. You claim no wood is ever dead,

even if it's gone to fire and risen as heat,
and think of them not as possessions but as guests
who will survive you, pass to other hands
the way they passed to yours. Sometimes a name
called out, a cough, a laugh will echo here—our voices
in the hollows of their bodies, for now, sustained.

Old English

I buried the sheepdog for you, trying
to save you from that grief, dug through muscled
roots, past rain-wet earth to harder, drier
soil that did not cling, but scoured the shovel.

Even the expected, smaller death recalled
the other. I transplanted sedum from the garden
to mark the place and obscure it.

Leave No Trace

We had driven past overlooks claiming
elevations of two, three thousand feet,
but there had been nothing to see and no one
but us to see it, moving through a cloud
that decided—frozen. But once above it,
we hiked into clearing air. Along
the Passamaquoddy, the falling fog
had left perfect white stockings on the trees,

an opalescent sheen on every surface.
Lichen, almost as old as the boulders
to which it cleaved, glowed gray and green
without the oppressive sun, and in places
puddled ice, milky, blind, still reflected
what the sky had been an hour ago. We cast
no shadow in that light. A narrow stream
still moved beneath its own freezing like the barest

pulse that persists a while after the breathing goes.
We ate our picnic on a rock ledge near it,
your breath crystallizing in your beard.
We would pack out all we brought—but talked
about how everyone fails in some
small way, our passage itself a slow,
collective wearing away of stone.
I told you I was relieved in such

failure, though the trace we left that day was
as intangible as what the raven's
        wing leaves behind it—moving space, downy
            sound—and brief as afterimage
                that vanishes to clear again, my eye
fixed on your back on the trail just ahead.

Buying the Painted Turtle

Two boys, not quite men, pretended to let it go
only to catch it again and again. And the turtle,
equally determined, each time gave
its heart to escape them. We were near
the base of the old dam where the river
became a translucent, hissing wall, fixed
in falling, where, by the size of it, the turtle
had long trusted its defense, the streaming

algae, green, black, red—the garden of its spine—
not to fail it. They held it upside down,
the yellow plastron exposed; they hoisted it
over their heads like a trophy. I left it
to you to do the bargaining, exchange
the money for us to save it, let it go;

fast, it disappeared into deeper
water, returning to another present,
where the boulders cut the current to cast
safer shadows of motionlessness. We were
already forgotten, then, like most gods
after floods recede, after fevers break.

We did not talk about what we had bought—
an hour, an afternoon, a later death,
worth whatever we had to give for it.